Versary

KATE LILLEY was born in 1960 and grew up in Perth and Sydney. After completing her PhD on Masculine Elegy at the University of London she spent four years as a Junior Research Fellow at Oxford University. Since 1990 she has taught feminist literary history and theory at the University of Sydney and has published widely on early modern women's writing and contemporary poetry. She is the editor of *Margaret Cavendish. The Blazing World and other writings* (Penguin Classics).

Versary

KATE LILLEY

PUBLISHED BY SALT PUBLISHING
PO Box 202, Applecross, Western Australia 6153
PO Box 937, Great Wilbraham, Cambridge PDO CB1 5JX United Kingdom

First published 2002

Printed and bound in the United Kingdom by Lightning Source

Typeset in Swift 9.5 / 13

British Library Cataloguing-in-Publication Data
A catalogue record for this book is available from the British Library
ISBN 1 876857 15 3 paperback

SP

1 3 5 7 9 8 6 4 2

: Melissa

Contents

Acknowledgments

Atlanta Review, Boston Review, Boxkite, Jacket, Literary Review, Meanjin, Overland, Poetry Review, Salt, Southerly, Southern Review, Stand. Fragments also survive in 'Sapphics' of poems published much earlier in *Cherwell, Final Taxi Review, New Poetry, Oxford Poetry, Scripsi* and *The Penguin Book of Modern Australian Poetry* eds John Tranter and Philip Mead (1991).

Calyx, ed. Michael Brennan and Peter Minter (Sydney: Craftsman House/Paperbark, 2000).

To my family and friends, and to Jean, my love and thanks.

*The places of memorie are resembled
unto Waxe and Paper. . . .
The utterance and using of them, is
like unto reading.*

WILSON'S *Art of Rhetorique* (1560)

Lady in the Dark

Nicky's World

As the plot rocks back and forth on a pinhead
count to fifteen very slowly.
By that time you should be alone again
contemplating your evening.

You could go for a ride and take a fall,
break your back and welcome an addiction -
or ask Miguel to serve drinks by the pool,
that hunky contractor might stop by.

Finally there's a knock at the door,
a lady policeman shows her badge.
She's asking if these unusual cufflinks
belong to the father of your children.

Souvenir

If the bones of the house appeal
build from appliance to the bowl your hands
position and empty, never lonely.
Amid snowstorms the day passes from me to you,
its scenes awash with love.
If I dream the tea cup your mother gave me
tears and I try to mend it with the wrong glue
it turns out the dream is teasing.
Let's go to Hawaii on our way to the Library of Congress.
How can I thank you for the pleasure of your company.

Block

The restored fountain churns pink bubbles
like a council-sponsored lounge act.

The police station next door looks like a toilet,
avant-garde and cruisy.

I'd like to stop and say hello at the old Thai
but the food at the new place is better.

If gays and lesbians don't shop at the gay
and lesbian bookshop who will?

The Korean bathhouse is great if you don't mind
running into students naked.

Quality Control

Formidable or freaked-out
make up your mind on the honeymoon

a turban creates a sense of occasion
over the holiday weekend

shop-soiled like a melamine tabletop
a yard sale soothes breach of promise

the working bee will reconvene
for an impromptu quiz

I'll supply the transcript
of a feud on the factory floor

Illocution

If I don't discontinue straight away
they'll put me in the other room and leave me.
I've been scouring the paper for tricks and misprints,
inserting silent letters where there are none.
A comprehension test with no prospect
of failure is a trial of parsimony.
If this were any other language
I'd turn in my office key and go home.

Arrest me now, I'm sick of it:
the subterfuge, the pain and suffering.
These stitches aren't the dissolving kind,
they'll need some caring, professional attention.
Discard, abolish, abrogate
explains desuetude if you're interested.

It follows

Resentment starts to go backwards in search of a new hermeneutic
the appointment slipped your mind that's no excuse

I'm the kind who'll sit in the waiting room and watch the second
    hand
for as long as it takes it's something I'm proud of I won't

leave just because it's dark outside and the street is slick with tears
it's impolite to tell you what you know already

and antisocial not to – I'll bounce back in a year or two
sorry there's no one on your side you'll have to take mine

no need to write that down I'll feel like a brute and it'll only fester
then we'll both be on our knees mewling and puking

it's the voice of a thousand gardens making me cranky and out of
    sorts
quit your dimwit hankering and hollering I don't want to hear it

Where Was I

High speed trains aren't meant for looking:
if you try to solve the blur you'll get a headache.
Masks are popular if you're feeling infectious
or prophylactically alert.
Sit back and practise mind-control instead,
turning the pages of a cartoon novel.
This one has pictures of lunch boxes emulating
regions and seasons, ingenious snacks
sold on certain days at certain stations.
Don't try to escape allegory
or over-read the vending machines.
You'll regret it later, and you'll miss a lot:
pre-mixed cocktails, blood-type fortunes,
bandaged schoolgirls shitting on Teacher.

1972

After the dance we cross the oval in pairs
to the steep bank behind the softball field.
The hall is bolted shut, teachers pass in the dark,
smoking and talking on the way to their cars.
It's cold on the ground, my buttons loose to the sky.

Panic Stations

I was rattled, shaken up
carbon dioxide making me reel

A bit of a crowd's gathering as I double over

I'm holding my breath on the bottom of the pool
horror's breaking through

I'll just sit here for a while

Sequel

Author v title in the sunken lounge
'abortion' in the index
  whose life am I living?
the blister platform is empty and so am I
rippled veneer
  feast and famine
a bracelet of lost charms
the blonde gleam of moonlight like a slide projector

When it comes to period pieces
genres get distressed
  and then everybody's anxious

Finally

quarto doesn't last a weak crush lingers
     like a festival of moss
the clerk of all passports takes me round
for a drink at a popular nightspot

I hear the voice-over from the start of Dirty Dancing
playing in the lounge and feel sedate
sedated
     like one more krispy kreme would set me up for life

if it's not one thing it's another
     if it's not your fault it's irrelevant
either way keep it sober
and sweet like some perpetual valentine

I read your letter o'er again
     it says what it doesn't say
for so long I've wanted you to be my pretty queen

Countrypolitan

Many words are falling you don't care
wasted lips forget and have some fun

each time you leave I make a vow
this will draw the line

thanks for something I can't win
heartache I can't use

I hate to admit the talk is true
my past is getting warmer while yours is growing old

someone new is crying in the most familiar way
I didn't do one wrong thing to you

Live at the Opry

Porter Wagoner in a nudie suit
flashes the crowd an embroidered *Hi!*
He kids around trading jokes with the hee-haw,
then the lights go down and the teardrops start.
The Queens of the Nashville Sound gear up,
nobody's laughing or chewing now.
Skeeter, frail in a sky blue sheath,
is out of rehab and born again.
Her voice has gone the way of her orchestra.
It's almost fifty years since the crash
that killed off the harmonising Davis Sisters,
the sleep-overs and double-dates,
square dancing after the Big Barn Frolic.
So long my honey, goodbye my dear,
gonna get along without you now.
When she holds the microphone to her lips
and whispers *mine is a lonely life*
it sounds like a radio tuned to the end of the world.

Screen

Take the road she took see where it goes

the strangest house on the block still stands
the little girl in the leaves is the love of my life

each blade of grass wrapped in gauze
commits our future happiness to memory

All this alleged wishing to be lucky

if you can't squander talent well what can you do
with this stack of change in your pocket

catastrophes can't be predicted only named in advance
everything means more than enough

Unsolved

volunteers fan out along the shore
the water's surface dimpled with flashlights

on the lake floor twisted in weed
the trail goes cold

the hinge of the locket a tiny sluice
one silver word

Lady in the Dark

Feudal conflict in a turn-of-the-century prep school leads to
    complications
for young lesbians and their guardians; an estate in litigation
    and a botched
paternity suit. When a daughter marries her mother's lover the
    air
fills with hieroglyphs, some you can see, others you can't
unless you're part of a certain clique of emotionally damaged
    outsiders.
Lucky for me I am and I love the Spanish interiors. What's next?
A musical about psychoanalysis starring Ginger Rogers in a tux
    and bow tie.
She's an editor who just *can't decide* (for example, should next
    month's cover
have a circus theme? No, of course not!). Instead of doing her
    job
she's dreaming up crazy dance routines in her dead mother's
    dresses.
It sounds a lot more enjoyable than it actually is but the couch is
    wild.
I pass the time fantasising about making-over my office
and thinking about the conventions of the Elizabethan stage.
In the case of the boy-heroine the umbrella of fiction was meant
    to fail.
Apparently Ginger needs a new lay-out and all the help she can
    get
from a truckload of smoke and mirrors, the spring line of Paris
    originals,
a deputy who won't roll over (Ray Milland) and a course of
    supervised
regression. *Is that all?* Cured after three sessions . . . Please! Call
    that *work*?
And where was the money changing hands? My mother loved
    Kitty Foyle
but she doesn't cut it as a mannish woman—or an analysand.

If the analyst had been more alluring—butch or femme or butch-
    femme,
a provocatively brainy woman of any kind, the whole thing
    juicier
and dubbed into Spanish, more alert to the complex nuances of
the therapeutic relation . . . well, I would say that, wouldn't I?

Formes Frustes

The two halves of a face should stay together
crying like doing the washing constantly
eventually they'll tire of the story of lithium
and give up on the miracles of science

there's every size and style of milk in the fridge
a rapid heartbeat *is* fear or might as well be
I'm three drinks behind my demented twin
and three ahead of the tab sorry and then some

Crime of Passion

The frame can't contain the enormity
of Lana Turner's chiselled head,
all that agitated recollection
colliding with the bliss of technicolour
in a series of lurid flashbacks.
Don't save your décolletage for a gala,
don't wait up in a palatial home.
According to you, a pathological liar,
the letter of apology is in the mail
with an autographed studio portrait.
Just as every drunk has a manuscript,
unlimited emotions need chemical assistance
to achieve a plateau of friendliness.
Blushing can be a mark of respect
but in this case I was past caring.
Anyone can get trigger-happy
with the right cocktail of provocation.
The body lands at the foot of the stairs
and inspires a Continental sojourn
with time-lapse photography and painted scenes
better than a ticket to the opera.

French Open

Request permission to shoot
the diamonds, the disasters.
The scene is changing by the minute.

Patio dining is a joke.
Paris clay is cruel.
No replays for you, nothing.

I'm going to leave you my coupons.
Shock, disgust, you know.
The waxworks are pricey but worth it.

What at first I thought was your home
was the garage and nothing special.
The big house is strictly off-limits.

Though the opening drags I stay
awake enjoying the tidal
wave of boredom and later

fondling her elegant breasts
genre grinds to a halt,
heedless of consequence.

In the Sun

Talk as long as you like,
the x-ray believes my story
is an anagram of yours.

I can put out the welcome mat
and sweep the dust away,
a storm of inference.

Let's be neoplatonic about it
and calculate our chances
for mutual admiration.

There's foreplay before the foreplay
and a backup of the backup.
I asked you here for a reason.

We made a verbal agreement
not to reproach ourselves
in the corner of a gentleman's club.

Then I told you of my suspicion
that fate had abandoned me
and wronged my station in life.

Hobohemia

As I brushed your arm and walked so close to you
I imagined meeting up with the author
of the classic statement on dance halls

When I asked about his research into bachelor communities
he answered interminably

Linda likes 36 boys 29 like her
the rest don't care for old time feeling
whipped preferably pussy anything
liberal touches of baby powder
just because I'm lonesome

You'll settle down some day and find I've gone away
all the fortune cookies equally cheerless
if you're passing by the doctor wants your blood
in exchange for a little morphine
it's not cheating just common sense

Birds start warbling bright and early
yonder a crash on the highway

I can't help it if the journey seems unreal
sure as I'm sitting here
the burden of the refrain will fall on me

say so

the figures are up across the board
the columns look sorry and feverish

if I memorise your reasons
I'll have to love them

in the meantime let me buy your initials
and afterwards change the locks

when the gauge is lit it's busier
so make a fire and evaporate

say when

even the blossoming tips of fruit trees
weep when they taste the exceptional flavour

that last aperitif was too much
I'll throw up the late harvest and ruin the season

are those two sisters now or were they ever
why don't you just shut up and run the test

when I bite through the striped seam of the gel cap
it is bitter to the nth degree

Mint in Box: A Pantoum Set

1

Doctors smoke for pleasure like everyone else
a gifted chassis lapsing into taste
busy accents cheapen off the rack
preamble loses mateship: bulk remorse

a gifted chassis lapsing into taste
when I see her in the past I mean imperfect
preamble loses mateship: bulk remorse
young designs for swift evacuation

when I see her in the past I mean imperfect
dress codes rule the shadow public sphere
young designs for swift evacuation
simple when your threshold was my library

dress codes rule the shadow public sphere
while libertines enjoy fraternity
simple when your threshold was my library
ornate to the point of infamy

while libertines enjoy fraternity
doctors smoke for pleasure like everyone else
ornate to the point of infamy
busy accents cheapen off the rack

2

Crushing petals in the lift is littering
sperm gets drowsy after five
fumbling the key like a villager
stranded in the vestibule

sperm gets drowsy after five
counting down to confession
stranded in the vestibule
my cunt ticks over the news

counting down to confession
fruitless pleasures rouse the family of perverts
my cunt ticks over the news
there are tears in the envelope

fruitless pleasures rouse the family of perverts
I'm glad
there are tears in the envelope
jealousy's daily ration

I'm glad
crushing petals in the lift is littering
jealousy's daily ration
fumbling the key like a villager

3

There's a knack to fixing the drapes
spring cleaning doesn't answer

unless you include prior convictions
reward me with infatuation

spring cleaning doesn't answer
sensitivity can't help suffering

reward me with infatuation
should that be complaint or compliant

sensitivity can't help suffering
creativity like a mock cheesecake

should that be complaint or compliant
the dictionary's asking

creativity like a mock cheesecake
don't do it to me or your parents

the dictionary's asking
how much warning is essential or desirable

don't do it to me or your parents
the ransom note explains the procedure

how much warning is essential or desirable
nil by mouth until morning

the ransom note explains the procedure
there's a knack to fixing the drapes

nil by mouth until morning
unless you include prior convictions

4

Canadians are crossing the Falls prescription in hand
customers don't want the Carry-on Luggage Act
attention is focussed on a blue house scaring the flowers
a dog biscuit has been placed on the casket in tribute

Customers don't want the Carry-on Luggage Act
her reputation was smeared across two states
a dog biscuit has been placed on the casket in tribute
can I watch you work, you've got a way with curls

Her reputation was smeared across two states
tips and butts for you girl, Goo-Goo Clusters
can I watch you work, you've got a way with curls
for Dollywood get off the bus at Knoxville

Tips and butts for you girl, Goo-Goo Clusters
I saw the stunt you pulled in the beauty parlour
for Dollywood get off the bus at Knoxville
that was the last piece of Lemon Icebox Sublime

I saw the stunt you pulled in the beauty parlour
the frozen girl's obituary is on file
that was the last piece of Lemon Icebox Sublime
my place is in the marble cemetery

The frozen girl's obituary is on file
it's your job to mop out the cubicles in the Love Art Shop
my place is in the marble cemetery
praise and blame as textual effects

It's your job to mop out the cubicles in the Love Art Shop
Canadians are crossing the Falls prescription in hand
praise and blame as textual effects
attention is focussed on a blue house scaring the flowers

5

Last time we met was so long ago I was straight
that could be a huge mistake for you and your client
weather cooperating
           it's a great day for comfort and convenience
if there were any injuries they have all been taken away

That could be a huge mistake for you and your client
dreams can cause heart attacks
           in infants with abnormalities
if there were any injuries they have all been taken away
it's your last chance to see the two spacecraft together

Dreams can cause heart attacks
           in infants with abnormalities
the word booty was used as in shake your booty
it's your last chance to see the two spacecraft together
a home invasion on a truly quiet block

The word booty was used
           as in shake your booty
sorority sisters are planning their next reunion
a home invasion on a truly quiet block
the retired fire captain knew what to do and did it

Sorority sisters are planning their next reunion
I guess I was not at my desk
           when your feelings changed
the retired fire captain knew what to do and did it
so far the trend is far more pills than men

I guess I was not at my desk
           when your feelings changed
take a seat and order something fancy
so far the trend is far more pills than men
the debt cannot be cancelled by any means

Take a seat and order something fancy
last time we met was so long ago I was straight
the debt cannot be cancelled by any means
weather cooperating
        it's a great day for comfort and convenience

6

Naturally formal qualities tax each moment
grief resembles superficially
desolate on occasion but not on all occasions
on the back of an envelope write the worst year of your life

Grief resembles superficially
filthy in other words is a persona
on the back of an envelope write the worst year of your life
you and the anecdote lost between non and ex

Filthy in other words is a persona
half-price at K-Mart guaranteed mint in box
you and the anecdote lost between non and ex
instinct maxes out and sleeps the weekend

Half-price at K-Mart guaranteed mint in box
here's a teaser—sounds like the fifties but isn't
instinct maxes out and sleeps the weekend
sick leave has to be taken before it expires

Here's a teaser—sounds like the fifties but isn't
compare and contrast identical pieces of writing
sick leave has to be taken before it expires
take your pick: sestina or double sestina

Compare and contrast identical pieces of writing
naturally formal qualities tax each moment
take your pick: sestina or double sestina
desolate on occasion but not on all occasions

7

Bob Hope is not dead
humidity is drying out
the Ritz may have asked employees to lie
    minivans in short supply

Humidity is drying out
girl impaled by metal rod
minivans in short supply
    bugs at famous resort

Girl impaled by metal rod
the IRS owes apologies and refunds
bugs at famous resort
    suspect goes berserk

The IRS owes apologies and refunds
Orlando should not be waving those flags in God's face
suspect goes berserk
    a grain elevator exploded Monday

Orlando should not be waving those flags in God's face
critics blast the mayor for having nothing better to do
a grain elevator exploded Monday
    more June than expected

Critics blast the mayor for having nothing better to do
Bob Hope is not dead
more June than expected
    the Ritz may have asked employees to lie

8

Each contestant must furnish a condo.
The reading list includes a choice of swimsuits.
Miss Teen USA wins a dark cherry Lincoln convertible.
Congeniality gets a gun shop and a White Castle franchise.
The reading list includes a choice of swimsuits.
Fern hillbillies seldom get their due.
Congeniality gets a gun shop and a White Castle franchise.
The man with a million friends denied himself.
Fern hillbillies seldom get their due.
I knew you were a decent person straight away.
The man with a million friends denied himself.
In convents you try to learn how things really are.
I knew you were a decent person straight away.
'I hate you,' Brenda shrieked, 'and so does Pedro'.
In convents you try to learn how things really are.
As a last resort the fixed income universe.
'I hate you,' Brenda shrieked, 'and so does Pedro'.
You don't want to drive all night for a piece of chocolate.
As a last resort the fixed income universe.
Under hypnosis blue entered her closet.
You don't want to drive all night for a piece of chocolate.
Each contestant must furnish a condo.
Under hypnosis blue entered her closet.
Miss Teen USA wins a dark cherry Lincoln convertible.

9

Mobile homes and substantial homes
brides with snake-handling hips
person to person ambition
sleeping and suffering less

Brides with snake-handling hips
self-saucing damsel damson
sleeping and suffering less
like sizing paper for a living

Self-saucing damsel damson
the big toe bends towards the pinkie
like sizing paper for a living
one of blood harmony's smart ideas

The big toe bends towards the pinkie
the shoes match the situation
one of blood harmony's smart ideas
an electrical grid mess on the ground

The shoes match the situation
lined up behind the information counter
an electrical grid mess on the ground
Easter Parade or My Fair Lady

Lined up behind the information counter
mobile homes and substantial homes
Easter Parade or My Fair Lady
person to person ambition

10

Walk towards me like a newsreel stuttering joy
a *catalogue raisonnée* of savant data
mechanical reproduction's on the skids
sign the card to receive your happy snap

a *catalogue raisonnée* of savant data
wilderness unfolding in your palm
sign the card to receive your happy snap
academics trading books for drugs

wilderness unfolding in your palm
events without witness draw their own conclusions
academics trading books for drugs
ask your scribbled questions curfew's knell

events without witness draw their own conclusions
mechanical reproduction's on the skids
ask your scribbled questions curfew's knell
walk towards me like a newsreel stuttering joy

Mid-century Eclogues

Your project is cool in the view-finder
emotional and spacious
feature walls of pebble and twine
assiduous pagodas

3-D refreshment takes its toll
like falling down at the shops
like being a swallow and singing about
owner-occupation

Convulsive spring's itinerary
of ranch-style innovation
tousled carpet crazy paving
meals all over the place

Indoor-outdoor luminescence
sentimental stripes
rugged comity of lawn
rhizome collateral

[Zinnia coquette]
Immense fluffy and ruffled six inches
across the loveliest zinnia
ever created its curved petals
resemble crysanthemums

A nest of tables is a talking point
when friends drop by uninvited
instead of making yourself a nuisance
pass the finger food

Tropes blend into the scheme in relaxing
instalments you'd hardly notice
I was hoping to reproduce the mood
of a brawl on the Champs Elysée.

Colour should be uninhibited and lend
a hand to the architecture
I had no idea how complicated
lingerie could be

Furniture clarifies itself
sexology's not kidding
guest bedroom is an oxymoron
rake the dirt if you want to

Hit the hay and hit it hard
overlook my faults
when the posse authorisation gets here
start deputising

Black Letter

The *most flourishing*
City in the World
is a ruinous Heap

The wrong Side *turned out*
makes *a* Doublet
of dumb Luck

Cinders *of* Diuturnity
black *Sparks*
Circumstances *indict* me

I'm going to *stay* Inside
and read *a* Book
until I feel like Myself

Ingression *of* antique Forms
the Scale *of* Influences
wearied

Be Chaste
in thy flaming Days
quadrate *and* consent

Rhetoric wherewith
I persuade
another Ear

I had the *ill* Fortune
to wear the Horns
I put them *in my* Pocket

Thickets *and* Brambles
girlish Ways
wishing *to be* a Slattern

So *it was* I began
to write my Sins
in Water

Early/Modern

In this strange labourinth how shall I turn?
Wayes are on all sids while the way I miss

MARY SIDNEY WROTH, *Pamphilia to Amphilanthus* (1621)

Circulating Library

1

The cure was energetic and left her restless
lasting pieces and toys flaked out in the vivarium

She could scarcely trust herself with the view
now that evening had advanced

Supper was animated and left her drained
she observed the casements
and had just strength to throw one open

Whispering echoes broken ground
she lay down on the mattress and thought no more

2

She seated herself in a chair near the lattice and yielded
she saw before her extended the very avenue
the locked gate at the end of the terrace
awakened mournful comparisons

She heard voices close at hand
the soft chimes of a young woman
and a man surely her tutor
describing the mineral and fossil substances
found in the depths of these mountains

3

The door opened at once into a dusky and silent chamber

She looked just as she had when she first came to the chateau
bringing news of the late extraordinary occurrence
her demeanour no less becoming and unaffected
than the snowy mounds peeking from the folds of her gown

The joy with which she received me
restored my tongue to its natural eloquence
I soon made her recollect our former intimacy

She personified the hour in the following lines

Spruce

As it says in the job description

Strew my clothes on the road leave me uninhabited

If you want my scribble and craving

Cancel my vendetta vanilla me

Dawdling chenille aphrodisiac

Bed as couch ok a valediction

Nymphomania's waning

You'll retire and buy a knighthood

Affect Ensemble

Silk tweed or satin toffee
twintone libido
at the water cooler

What comes after ash blonde?
custard donut or covered button
air conditioning or brandy alexander

You can scan my glowing interior
and write down what you see there
thou hast curiously embroydered me

Like a safe in a hotel wall
like the keys to the city
be my guest

Lady-in-waiting

a batch of defective miniatures
wet 'n' dry shitloads of themed anthologies
the going rate for scribal publication

an imaginary critics' circle
collates the known variants and picks up the tab
when hospitality goes wrong

the lodgings have no charm and no bar
the mistress of cheap rooms is punctual to a fault
topos of excessive suffering and detail

patron of the afternoon in a tailored costume
the conduct books have a word for it
sprezzatura of the feminine vernacular

Georgic

The waterfall attracts its share of losers.
Nearby flowers recite past favourites unselfconsciously,
bowing their heads to the grass as the mercury falls.
Jocund and lowing abreact,
whistling charms the furrows.
The aesthetics of picnics gather parks
and trays embossed with birds and branches.
Lunch is served in the royal enclosure
by costumed swains and youths glad of the work.
Dishevelled planets grow up in arrears
and shed their light like imported brocade
used in the manufacture of evening bags.

As Is

Lonely stairway not so long ago
a raincoat's floral lining

local girls trying seconds and samples
no exchange or refund

chiasmus of symptom and side effect
flooding chemical debris

strophe and antistrophe in the garment district

Tender

You promised the trip would enthrall me
like a sexually liberated cousin recto verso

decency comes forward
a museum of sorts

the adroit prospect stalls
retrieval of buxom ephemera

misdemeanours vie in the channels of noise
my assignment thorough disgrace

daily usage hastens
beauty's senseless dewpoint

I'll flip you for the password sorrowfully
as if I were the Queen of Sweden newly minted

Starry Messenger

Mouthfuls of shame like an understudy
subigatrix voyage

my melody
my novelette
my secret solar system

courier of lightning's borrowed oeuvre
strolling fricatrice

Post

Take it back
sure I'm lapping it up
well and truly eaten

Never let the sun go down
gorgeous or not

Spackle what you can't amortise
solder clues
seal the flap

Discipline has the pleasant voice
of virtue in distress

Can modernism get any later?
Is it my turn to paddle forgone Niagara
barreling into nowhere?

Anamorphosis

For starters it's vexatious
a meritocracy

you might look like her
she might look like me

undulating brunette fixation
melting depositary

backyard wreck and salvage
mount of piety

Mock-Tudor

Medieval recreation: who'd have thought
tournaments of swing

like the Plague, like the Great Fire
anniversaries keep happening

interregnum of legendary statues
the perfect pitch of masquers in the wonder cabinet

genitals speak posthumously
in the form of an oracle

the crossed-out lyric subject circa 1590
my Anacreontic cupid, boon companion

you'll know what I mean by agitation
outraged or moist or both

Tragicomedy

Industry bribes Melancholy
to monitor shifts between genre and mode,
    georgic and pastoral.
What I've heard of Volume 1 is bucolic,
a twisted *roman à clef.*

The judging panel wants consensus,
a mixture of peer review and graft
    more lyric than dramatic.
The conversation won't leave the room
without a chaperone.

Fees allude to the structure of romance,
a plan to continue metaphor
    by extending a line of credit.
It's ruin for some, reparation for others.
What did you expect?

Prosopopoeia

It used to drain a lot out of me—
              having your own problems and dealing with
      someone else's pain.
Who has the energy after work?

Stick the headphones on and wake up later,
      the fan whirring in the background.

Give me therapy-without-insight any day,
              mood disorders shimmering like a wash of colour
      or customised tint,
part of the decor I can live with.

I don't need to know how it works or answer stupid questions:
      do you feel safe, does orgasm matter?

It's like homework reciting abandonment
          my cv as novel or epitaph:
      "I would rather be somebody's darling
than a poor girl nobody knows".

      The thought of continuous assessment drags.

Isn't it clear which characters are ghosts?

Synecdoche

(for SJW)

We take up too much space
five of us in a room for twenty

like children on detention
who will never meet again

Susan brings bone china smudged with newsprint
from a junk shop on the way

when I hold the bowl to the light
we can see our hands through the milky ground

The anaesthetist slides on a plastic glove
enters to the elbow and says it's big

tomorrow I'll wake in a mask
nothing and no one

Historic

We had a little fuss today
over a bunch of gowns.
There's no call for them anymore,
not this century.
I was down on the floor waxing,
steady as a metronome.
I go deaf when I'm concentrating.
I'm not buying I'm collecting,
that way we'll get along.
Ave atque vale,
stranger remember me.
Mostly it's a horoscope.

Preterition

It's your prerogative to greet me in a blameless spotlight
my lofty and messed up stuff in a chorus of frost

sooner or later we'll be better off
less puffy, more stuck together

conventions come to me, an enduring regime
a swapmeet for humans and non-humans

inhibitions sensible and carnal
instant stimulation with which with whom

Elegy

The less you say
the more I love you
the other way round

dear object
I am your proxy
thing of the past

propinquity in cameo
freaked analogy
double fugue

the flower list in sequence
flawless decade
what a *dust*

Envoy

Diplomatic method
counting back to one
the to and fro of jilted information

leave me the grief you said goodbye to
its exemplarity
parcel and part

Sapphics

Time hath endless rarities, and shows of all varieties

THOMAS BROWNE *Urn-Burial* (1658)

Axioms

Transference fucks with your head

Forgetfulness makes you face facts

Exhilaration leads to debt

RENOWNED INTRODUCTIONS | WOOLLEN MATERIAL

FASCINATION SALON

The vanishing *SOLIDA Non-plus-ultra Hairnet* with Transpa-Knit
makes all other hairnets obsolete

Suddenly little bullets explode
you're an open target for anything

What you see in the rear-vision mirror isn't normal

Chicken thigh schnitzel
compact indulgence
a motivational piece of skirt

Three o'clock is the hour when Jesus died for you and me

Blank screen | Still face

Afternoons are slow parataxis is painful
prolepsis and analepsis
picaresque and episodic

Preference and orientation
        are the same thing aren't they?

it's a puzzle for elocution
        and lyric infrastructure

Deep discount
double depression
extreme unction

I saw you cross the lights at Elizabeth and Park
        thought twice

G'DAY SUSHI & TOBACCO | SELF-STORAGE

AUSCRAP

plate 2
glasses 3
rabbit 3
_____
8

Our Lady of the Snows

Leaves that used to slip past
stick in my hair like thorns

I wander down to the dock
like a stranger just on shore

My fingers are knotted joint to joint
they cannot reach the latch

Who else lies awake in the building?
who sleeps each night in the same arms?

At dawn the fingerprint men
search the yards of decommissioned stock

The bride hovers skimming veined marble
over her head the flags unfurl
their international standards

Nymph of our garden she surfaces
as the froth on some distant fountain
in Arethusa or the Hesperides

Precision-timed explosions create
acres of visual illusion

Light up your album of beautiful sights

Notes

"Nicky's World" is the name of a collector's plate commemorating the long-running American soap opera, *The Young and the Restless*.

"Sequel." Susan Stewart's 'Notes on Distressed Genres', *Crimes of Writing*, Oxford University Press, 1991, ch.3, has left its mark on this poem.

"Finally" borrows its title and last line from the Wayne Walker/Mel Tillis song of the same name. Recorded as a duet by Kitty Wells and Webb Pierce it went to #9 on the country charts in 1964.

"Countrypolitan" recycles some words and phrases from hits of the 50s recorded by Ray Price aka the Cherokee Cowboy. Countrypolitan was what happened to the Nashville Sound in the late 60s and 70s: honky-tonk voices matched with lush pop productions and urban lyrics, exemplified by the cross-over appeal of Tammy Wynette.

"Live at the Opry" uses some titles and lines from the Skeeter Davis songbook: "The End of the World", "Gonna Get Along Without Ya Now" and "Mine is a Lonely Life". Mary Frances Penick took the name Skeeter Davis from her schoolfriend and singing partner, Betty Jack Davis. Picked up by Chet Atkins, the Davis Sisters had a #1 hit with 'I Forgot More Than You'll Ever Know' in 1953-4. Driving back from the Wheeling, West Virginia Jamboree on August 1 Betty Jack was killed in a head-on collision, Skeeter was driving. When Skeeter returned to recording as a solo artist in 1957, double-tracked vocals, duets of one, became her signature. Colin Escott comments in his notes for *The Essential Skeeter Davis* (RCA), "Skeeter was one of the original 60s girl groups". She has been a core performer at the Opry since the late 50s, where the live to air shows (now partly televised) are interspersed with ads for chocolate Goo-Goo Clusters, ubiquitous in Nashville.

Formes Frustes. "[M]ultifaceted syndromes can appear in incomplete forms – what Freud, in his discussion of anxiety neurosis, called 'rudimentary' or 'larval' presentations of the illness, or illness-equivalents, and what are now most often called *formes frustes*", Peter Kramer, *Listening To Prozac*, Viking Penguin, 1993, 197. Two chapters of *Listening To Prozac* concern *formes frustes*.

"Crime of Passion" responds to the 1966 version of the melodrama, *Madame X*, starring Lana Turner.

"Hobohemia" is a coinage borrowed from Nels Anderson's Chicago School study, *Hoboes: A Sociology of Homeless Men*, University of Chicago Press, 1922. I encountered this reference in Kevin J. Mumford, *Interzones. Black/White Sex Districts in Chicago and New York in the Early Twentieth Century*, Columbia University Press, 1997.

"Crushing petals" uses some leading words and tropes from Foucault's *History of Sexuality*, Volume 1.

"Miss Teen USA". "Fern hillbillies" is a term used to describe the often-overlooked women singers associated with "ol' timey" country music, including largely forgotten female duets like the Coon Creek Girls.

"Starry Messenger". *Starry Messenger (Sidereus nuncius*, Venice, 1610) is the title of a treatise by Galileo announcing the telescopic discovery of the satellites of Jupiter. Subigatrix—from subigate, to knead or work up—and fricatrice—from *fricre*, to rub—are early modern words used to denote a "lewd woman", especially one who engages in improper, sodomitical (ie nonprocreative) contact with other women. Jonson's *Volpone* (1605) speaks of "a lewd harlot, a base fricatrice". The OED doesn't gloss the lesbian implications of "rubbing" and "kneading".

"Prosopopoeia", speaking in character. The Dorsey Dixon song, "Wreck on the Highway", was recorded by the Louvin Brothers, perhaps the greatest of all country duos, in 1962.

"Elegy". The phrase, "dear object", is taken from Katherine Philips' "Orinda to Lucasia parting, October 1661, at London".

Printed in the United Kingdom
by Lightning Source UK Ltd.
103655UKS00001B/194